Tango

Tango

Poems by

Terry Godbey

© 2025 Terry Godbey. All rights reserved.
This material may not be reproduced in any form, published,
reprinted, recorded, performed, broadcast,
rewritten or redistributed without
the explicit permission of Terry Godbey.
All such actions are strictly prohibited by law.

Cover design by Shay Culligan
Cover image by Getty Images on Unsplash+
Author photo by Bob McComas

ISBN: 978-1-63980-777-2

Kelsay Books
502 South 1040 East, A-119
American Fork, Utah 84003
Kelsaybooks.com

*for Bob, who dropped back into my life
after 44 years
and brought his guitar*

*and for Claire, who cares about each word
almost as much as I do*

Acknowledgments

I am grateful to the editors of the following magazines and anthologies in which versions of these poems appeared or are forthcoming:

Aquifer: The Florida Review Online: "Upon Googling an Old Boyfriend and Finding His Obituary"
Autumn Sky Poetry DAILY: "Ordinary Hours"
Chameleon Chimera: An Anthology of Florida Poets: "Finding Love at 66"
Crosswinds Poetry Journal: "Final Hearing"
Green Hills Literary Lantern: "The Great Tit," "I Decide to Stop Being a Victim"
Passages North: "The Girls' Social Calendar Fills Up"
Rosebud: "Hanging the Moon"
Slipstream: "First Date," "If I Dare," "Lemonade," "Friday Nights at the Skating Rink," "Mortal"

Contents

Why I Gave Up Men	13
Final Hearing	15
First Date	17
I Decide to Stop Being a Victim	19
The Girls' Social Calendar Fills Up	21
The Great Tit	23
My Safari Guide	24
I Can't Remember	26
Kinetic Energy	28
This Is Not a Country Song	29
Someone New	31
Postcard	33
Finding Love at 66	34
Dare	35
Fever	36
The Promise	38
Hanging the Moon	41
Mortal	43
Ordinary Hours	47
Aperture	49
City of Doors	51
Upon Googling an Old Boyfriend and Finding His Obituary	53
Lemonade	55
Mints	57
Friday Nights at the Skating Rink	59
If I Dare	61

This world is half farewell, half embrace.
    —Laura Paul Watson

Why I Gave Up Men

> *I was tired of being a woman,*
> *tired of the spoons and the pots,*
> *tired of my mouth and my breasts,*
> *tired of the cosmetics and the silks.*
>   —Anne Sexton

I was tired of being a wife,
a girlfriend, a lover,
an object of desire,
tired of falling
from my pedestal,
tired of running men off
with my broom.

I was tired of men
who needed to be coddled,
tired of broken promises
and bickering, of pretending,
of losing pieces of myself,
of shaving my legs
every damn day,
tired of feeling
like a performing monkey
in bed, tired of parroting *I love you*'s
I no longer felt.

I stopped trusting pleasure,
no longer chased it. Then came
The Year of Absolutely No Pleasure,
a fiery three-car pileup of cancer,
divorce and job loss. When I climbed out
of the wreckage, barely alive, I clung

to my remission, my diminished body,
ecstatic to awaken each morning
strong enough to leave my bed.
It seemed natural then to break free
of my addiction to men,
whom I had considered
as essential as ice cream,
without the calories,
for most of my life.

I waved away offers
to set me up, steered clear
of dating websites, decided men
brought drama but little else.
In place of desire, I wanted
no entanglements,
no obligations, clean lines,
tranquility, precious hours
off work that belonged only to me.

If Jackson Browne had rung
my doorbell, I would have
changed my tune.
Alas, he did not.

Final Hearing

In the last hours of our marriage,
I threw open the courthouse doors
to an array of armed guards
and a sullen crowd
winding through rows of steel guide rails.

Then I saw you
two lines ahead.

It was impossible
not to meet your eyes
each time we passed
on our slow approach
to the metal detector.

The judge questioned
our long separation—
I explained your gift
of health insurance—
and he congratulated us,
me for my remission,
you for your kindness,
pronounced us
ex-husband and wife.

We waited side by side
for our official decrees.
You offered to lend me the fee
when I fumbled for my wallet.

I did not expect
such a crush of regret
after so much time apart.

I did not expect us to move close
only to drift apart again
in a grim morning promenade
along the marble floors
like the back and forth
between distance and affection
of our 25 years.

I did not expect us
to park near each other by chance
in the massive garage,
where you climbed into your car,
I got into mine and we opened
our windows to release
the bottled-up heat, drove off
beneath a savage sun.

First Date

Suddenly single
and I'm blasting off
in a speedboat
with a man
so Old World handsome and muscled
I want to remove his swimsuit
with my teeth. What scenery!

We start slow,
glide with motor in idle
through a mile
of swampy canal.
Egrets startle
and take wing—flashes
of white light—
a turtle tips
off its log, great
blue herons skulk
among the bald cypress.

When we enter the swollen
lake, we pick up speed,
my new hat blows away.
I can't stop laughing.
We drop anchor, share
a bottle of Chardonnay,
swim. He helps me back
onto the boat, finally
we touch,
but he gives me

a friendly peck on the cheek,
no bedroom eyes
or innuendo.

So this
is my new life.
The only things rising
are a mean sun
and my blood.

I Decide to Stop Being a Victim

Try not to make too much of suffering.
Try not to make it into a profession.
—Tony Hoagland

First, I try releasing my anxiety
little by little,
a flock of balloons
rising over the lake,
the gold lust
of orange blossoms
and wild orchids
painting my pale skin.

For a year, I wore
a *Kick Me* sign
but now it's time.

I hold a pillow over her face
until she stops thrashing,
force her head underwater
until bubbles dance
to the surface.
I poison her
the way she poisoned me.
I murder her
before she can murder me.

Good riddance
to the trembling,
bug-eyed horror,
the nausea and pain
that etched my face.

The cancer
was vanquished.
The spooked woman
looking over her shoulder
is gone for good.
I know
because I watched her die.

The Girls' Social Calendar Fills Up

Not long after surgery,
another suspicious area
lights up my mammogram
and magnifies
my attachment
to my attachments.

There are none like them
anywhere! Cushiony,
flushed, alive.
Pale pink areolas.
Sweet button nipples.

Can I live
without them?

A week later, the news—
still in remission!
Time to celebrate,
show them off
with strands of shiny beads
at Mardi Gras,
take them dancing
in a scoop-necked red dress—
the tango, of course.

I'll turn each day
into a décolletage adventure.

I'll flash the mailman,
grocery bagger,
toll-booth operator.

What fun I'll have
in rush-hour traffic.

The Great Tit

Back at work
a week after the third biopsy,
my shish-kabobbed boob
swollen to twice its normal size,
I flip through
the pages I missed
on my Bird-a-Day calendar,
arrive at today's feature:
THE GREAT TIT!

Damn, cancer can crack a joke!

My laugh is no more musical
than the great tit's song,
which the calendar compares to a squeaky saw.
I cut loose with my own racket
somewhere between a madwoman's cackle
and the shrieks of an exotic parrot,
paroxysms of pleasure
loud enough to almost erase
the memory of the long needles,
the pinch of the clamp, the creep factor
of the cold metal table
with a hole for my breast
raised above the radiologist's head

but mostly in honor
of irony, wit
and my own great tit.

My Safari Guide

He was on a hunting expedition
of his own, approached me
at a wildlife viewing area
at Animal Kingdom.
It was early,
the tourists sleeping off
last night's Pretoria Punch.
Zebras tore at the grass,
giraffes breakfasted on treetops.

I kept my eyes on the savannah,
narrowed through the viewfinder,
seeing only what I chose to see,
yet we clicked.
He threw questions pointed as tusks,
surprised by my candor
about my illness, my divorce—
American adventures.

You're so strong, he said.
Come to the Kalahari.
I'll take you on a real safari,
show you things
you won't believe.

Later, at the pool,
waiting for my sleeping-in son,
I went exploring
to find the source
of exotic bird calls

and there was my safari guide
half hidden among the banana trees.

*I'm really interested in you
and I'm not afraid to say it,*
he said. *Why don't you move
to Botswana with me?
We'll marry and be a happy
family.*

*I think you're a little young
for me,* I said.
I don't care about that,
he said. *I like you
just the way you are.*
I did the math: 23 years.
Hmmm.

I put down my camera, looked
at him, hard. He didn't appear
to be kidding, grabbed my phone
and punched in his number.

I didn't say, *That's ridiculous.*
I didn't say, *What if my cancer comes back?*
I didn't say, *I don't know you,
and you don't know me.*

I said,
I'll think about it.

I Can't Remember

for Bob

You were a friend
44 years ago, an echo
of your new status as boyfriend,
and now that you're back
you're dredging the mucky lake
for old memories,
occasions I've forgotten.
It's true, I can't remember
teaching you to play "Take It Easy"
on guitar, showing you how to turn
a box of spaghetti into saucy magic,
singing along with you
at a Fleetwood Mac concert,
calling you first
after I fell asleep at a red light
and smacked the car
in front of me.

You floated back to me
through the decades
with precise remembrances
and are not pleased
about all my gaps,
understandably,
especially about the two hours
we spent whooping it up
on the wide wooden porch
of a riverfront hotel,
and I think perhaps my memory

has always been poor
though I probably forgot that trait
along with many other things
you remind me I've forgotten.

No matter what happens
with us in the weeks ahead
I promise to never forget
the moment you appeared
at my door, auburn curls gone gray,
how you turned my weekends
into kayaking capers
and all-night guitar jams,
the revelations of your lips,
your pond-blue eyes pulling me in
and how utterly safe
and cherished I feel
wrapped in your king-sized limbs.

Kinetic Energy

I've gone 10 days
without seeing my new man
and now there's a delay
of five more.
Could his absence
actually kill me?
It feels possible
though as a cancer survivor
I know that sounds ridiculous.
He's four states away
on an emergency trip,
and our distance cuts deep.
No medicine can help me
with my own emergency
for he is the drug
I need, his skin and lips,
the fierce, familiar surge
that electrifies our weekends,
hearts seesawing,
producing enough kinetic energy
to power a small town.
I like to think all this energy
from our bodies in motion
is renewable
and cannot be destroyed
but with every day he's away
I'm less certain.

This Is Not a Country Song

All I've ever learned from love
is how to shoot somebody
who outdrew you.
        —Leonard Cohen

Do you dare go full-bore?
It's the only way
to know for sure,
but I feel you decelerating,
becoming stolid
like a riverbank
while I long to be lashed
by the current, dodging rocks,
not minding a few bruises,
attracted, as always, to risk.

There are four of us
when we're alone:
Our pasts squeeze between us
on the sofa, crouch behind
the seats in your van.
They ramble on
about our foibles,
remind us
where the bodies are buried.
Their clatter drives me mad.

This is not a country song,
but we both know I'm unreliable
when tedium begins to gnaw.
No one has ever left me;

perhaps that's part of the problem.
Maybe you'd like to be the first.
Or could it be we're in love
with the idea of love,
believe it's our last chance.

I promise to never lie to you,
and you have to trust me.
This is not a country song
but the way I see it
our path ahead comes down to this:
I can't fall
if you won't go there with me.
I can't play
if you're not in the game.
So choose—
carnal evenings
or more carnage?

Someone New

When I stroke your strong
legs in our jumble of sheets,
memorizing the rise
of your calves,
I'm also studying
my own reflection.
I'm someone new with you.
My mistakes recede
until I can almost pretend
they never happened.
The tattered years,
the other men,
fade away.

Before you, I traded a double life
for no life. I traded the whisper
of innuendo for silence.
For 10 long years,
I forgot how to dream.
Now I can be honest,
nothing to hide,
free to unchain my longings,
rabid and raw.

When you glide your fingers
along my curves,
I feel my life rushing through,
yours filling me, spilling.
I've cupped my hands around
so much of this world

and tried to grab hold
but it was never enough.

There's so much you don't know
about our decades apart
I have room to shape-shift,
to try on other personas,
maybe one who doesn't flee
at the first sign of friction,
a woman with faith.

Postcard

Summer evening, cool sheets
smooth and waiting, my only visitor
the porch light moth.

Again I glance at the postcard
from Greece, guess he won't arrive
tonight, maybe not next week.

More than ocean separates us,
reminders turn into torment:
moonstone ring, mountain tea

with lemon, indelible press
of chest and thighs, each long night
unrelenting reprise.

Was it not what it seemed,
the simple life in the hilltop house,
bright blue shutters,

the courtyard where I read
under the olive tree's
silvery leaves? From the terrace

rimmed with geraniums
he called me back to bed—
we fed each other bread

and wine, tree-ripened figs
from Marrakesh, each long night
seeds pulled from flesh.

Finding Love at 66

*Maybe there is nothing, ever,
that can equal the recollection
of having been young together.*
          —Michael Cunningham

I opened the Facebook message and out came
an old friend

I opened the old friend and out came
a man who fell for me decades ago

I opened the man who fancied me without my notice and out came
someone who knew me better at 22 than I knew myself

I opened the confidante with whom I had been young—out came
an outdoorsy photographer who radiated a quiet kindness

I opened that kindness and attention and out came
a supercharged version of myself whose skin began to dance

I opened my skin to his and we became
a spray of sparks, starflash and second chances

Dare

Have you ever been so unraveled
by a kiss
you wanted to be swallowed
whole?

Or lost yourself in a lover's eyes,
seen everything you desire there
and just as quickly
all of it spinning away?

Have you wondered how much of memory
is made of wishes, knots
in a row, a rope you'll climb
until your final, ragged breath?

Have you been humbled
before the sky spritzed with stars,
pleaded with Sirius
to teach you patience?

Do you dare search
the underbelly of your dreams
for the answers
to what haunts you, regrets

spread out like bleached bones,
your vast restlessness
a pond sleeping
before the next stone?

Fever

In the wee hours,
I sense you beside me,
reach out, am startled awake
by chilled sheets, your absence,
a jarring emptiness
filling me.

Then I remember:
You are sick with COVID
40 miles to the east,
in a bed with a view of a river
the color of old nickels,
fever lapping the shores
of your skin. We have broken
our weekend spell, unable to touch.

But five days ago, we touched.
You tested negative then
so I made chicken soup, massaged
your legs and feet, kept the cups
of hot tea coming, nursed
what we thought was a bad cold.

Now it seems you might have shared
the virus with me. I cough
and sniffle, rock between burning up
and freezing, try not to touch
my swollen lymph nodes,
wait to see how sick I'll become
without, as my doctors say,
much of an immune system.

I wish the soup weren't gone,
keep company with books,
movies, and a neon green parrot
whose bright eyes watch me
lie still on the sofa. He wonders
when you will arrive, when the guitars
will be brought out of their cases.

Ah, but there will be no music today,
no healing through fingertips,
no skin against skin, dissolving
of selves, blending of boundaries.
We are divided by circumstance,
necessity.

I shiver,
relax into the embrace
of a velvety blanket
even as the walls swell
and contract like a bellows,
a shimmer of heat
distorting all the edges.

The Promise

Surely no one was ever so eager
to go, so ready for the unknown,
so fearless, bone-tired,
emphatically sick
of the needles,
catheters and cuffs,
beeping machines
and their damning numbers,
flashing lights and alarms
no nurse would do a damn thing about
because for them
it was all COVID all the time
and anyone with the audacity
to try to die of old age
must fend for herself.

My mother moaned with every exhalation,
seven hours of pain and sorrow
as we waited for her last ride,
to hospice. I rushed past
the COVID patients
laid out in the hallway
and pressed the nurses,
if I could find any,
to hurry the ambulance.
Mom cried out in pain
when I tried to hold her hand,
mumbled greetings to her long-gone
mother, father, grandson
but still she stayed with me,

bound to her body,
bound to her emergency room bed,
though eager to be numb,
to float in nothingness, to be dumb,
for all the words had been spoken:
Hospice, hospice, hospice.
I soothed her: *Any minute,
I promise.*

And when finally
two ambulance attendants arrived
to take her to that dim place
of kindness and limitless morphine,
she said her last words:
Thank you, Terry.
Her breathing eased,
she grew calm.
The men removed her IV
and wheeled her out,
the sacred moment
my stubborn mother began to leave
her life behind.
She had refused to die
in that undignified ER
and without getting her way
one last time.
Her eyes never opened
in the hospice room
she had wished for so ardently,
but I like to think its peace
and tenderness beckoned to her
because she went quickly, quietly.

She did not simply vanish
and leave all of us
to go on as before
as if death were a bookmark.
I am learning what people mean
by *the hard work of grieving*.
It's a place I visit often,
reliving her final hours,
dreaming up scenarios
where she arrived at hospice sooner,
where I didn't let her down.

I decided my mother needed
one final trip,
to her beloved Maine hometown,
and I tucked her high school photo
into my camera bag
so she would see
everything I saw:
autumn leaves littering the trail,
boats bobbing along the waterfront,
the graves of her parents
in sight of the fire station
where her father had ruled as chief,
the lobster pound, the park
where she had whiled away
long summer afternoons
picking wild raspberries
in her youth.

It was there
I said goodbye.

Hanging the Moon

I'm six weeks old, all in white
like a lamp in my mother's lap,
her mother and grandmother beside us,
gloomy in dresses of dark cotton,
pin-curled and bespectacled,
not a smile among us.

A baby, I'm expected to be cranky,
but why do they look so sour
in the black-and-white photo?
Maybe my great-grandmother was fretting
about her husband, who wouldn't go to church,
was over-fond of whiskey.
Perhaps my grandmother was cooking up
her next wisecrack, intended to rile
her new son-in-law.
And what was my mother thinking?
Only 21, a fresh-faced party girl
who might never have married
her Air Force fling if not
for the complication of me.

First child, first grandbaby,
all that power I held
in my tiny fists,
three generations of women
attuned to my every twitch.
All that love.
Whatever I wanted,
they would give me.

After a year, we moved away
but I still felt the pull
of Belfast, Maine,
and my grandmother,
and for her I hung the moon.
Our summer visits began with good cheer,
a frenzied release
from back-seat Auto Bingo
with my brother and sister,
but before long, my mother turned sullen,
my father began leaving the room,
grumbling that Nana doted on me,
ignored my siblings.

In the photo, I'm gazing straight ahead
while my ancestors glance
to the side, as if glimpsing the future,
an unpleasantness to come,
in their faces a resignation
I saw every time we cut short another visit
and piled into our station wagon,
my grandparents waving from the sidewalk
until we turned the corner,
my parents' eyes trained on the road.

All those grand ladies are gone,
my mother only five months ago.
She never really knew me
and now it's too late.
All that love.
All that power I held.
Whatever I wanted, they would give me.
Except the thing I needed.

Mortal

I couldn't breathe
but couldn't bring myself
to dial 911
maybe because the last time I did that

I shot straight to the asthmatic brink
—a chilled, blue void
the color of my face—
and then ICU psychosis was unmasked

when the Phantom of the Opera
danced nightly
to the beat of the beeps.
This time I thought, *just a bad cold,*

in retrospect a poor decision
I'm partly blaming on the scarcity
of oxygen in my blood.
As the asthma compressed my chest,

I stayed calm at the window
watching ruby-throated hummingbirds
visit my feeder. Three inches long,
impossibly miniature, their immense

energy needs keep them perched
on the border of life and death,
a delicate, dangerous balance.
Their wings beat 80 times a second

and they need nectar every 15 minutes.
I haven't felt like eating and have no energy.
Breathing takes every bit of stamina
I can muster. I should get a trophy

for descending my stairs to watch
the hummers from my front porch.
Some say the birds are a sign
the spirit of a loved one

is near, maybe my mother, saying,
You should have called 911.
A hummingbird sighting can also signal
tough times are over and healing

can begin. I want to believe that.
A bee sting can kill a hummingbird
because they are so small,
tinier than many dragonflies,

needy, burdened, bursting,
shimmering with iridescence,
the only birds that don't flap their wings
but rotate them in all directions,

the reason they can hover,
fly backward and upside down.
When one leaves my feeder,
its acrobatic flight is so swift

I can't follow its path, a zipper
that never snags, a hologram
melting into the morning sky.
I imagine there's a nest nearby

with eggs the size of coffee beans.
The neighborhood red-shouldered hawk
came in low and circled
while a hummingbird sipped. Hawks

are said to not bother with hummers
because there's not enough meat
for the effort, but I got a hit of adrenaline,
helpful in my condition, and was ready to fight

till it glided away over the treetops.
I was too ill to drive myself across town
but my doctor granted a virtual visit,
threw out the phrase *medical emergency*,

ordered a battalion of meds and told me
to call 911 if my oxygen saturation dipped
to 90. It went down to 89. Technically,
I did as I was told. Once I am well again,

I'll slide on my fetching new nectar ring
with its red plastic flower and wait
for a hummingbird to approach my hand.
They are very curious and I am, too.

I want to see one up close, hear it hum.
My son is bringing groceries any minute.
I'll force myself to eat
because even though this precarious dance

along the edge is agonizing and slow,
I am drawing breath after breath
of glorious oxygen and craving
the rich but finite syrup that infuses my days.

Ordinary Hours

Cradled in my hammock,
I watch clouds scud past
like a movie in which the director is drunk.

A whirling copper sun
with spinning crystals
splashes my newspaper
with rainbows as I read
about Buzz Aldrin,
ever the optimist,
celebrating his 93rd birthday
by taking his fourth wife.

Think of it! To walk on the moon—
the MOON—then return
only to weather
mundane disappointments
and sticky divorces
like any mortal.
How could anything on Earth
measure up
after stepping foot on the lunar surface?

Sparkle, flash
and otherworldly intensity enrich us—
but for now I'll take
these ordinary hours.
All day, planes inscribe
the chalky, blue slate,
wind chimes clank

their clumsy songs,
a counterpoint
to the cooing
of mourning doves
preparing for sleep
as evening comes on
languid as syrup, the sky
in its vibrant last flush,
my love beside me
in the cushiony air,
where nothing happens
and absolutely everything happens
as we wait for the moon
and the planets
to switch on their lamps
one by one.

Aperture

*Bokeh—The visual quality of the out-of-focus parts
of a photograph, which draws our attention
to a particular area of the image.*

How much light?
I open it all the way,
try for luminous, vibrant,
no muted colors, quiet pastels,
creep close to my subject,
choose shallow depth of field
for the rich bokeh,
the way the playground looked
from the merry-go-round.

That's how I see the last 50 years,
a rushing wash of color,
made lovelier by blur,
a few hundred days in sharp focus
with scrapbook captions—
*Picking out lobsters in Bar Harbor,
Tyler's first swim in the ocean,
our favorite trail in the Rockies—*

but tens of thousands of days
either forgotten
or smoothed and smudged
until unremarkable
and dozens of desperate days
chosen for special treatment,
to be mulled over

and poured into poems
like soufflé molds,
to be baked for years
into books
people actually pay for
though I pay more, and keep paying,
my mistakes
only a little less monstrous
on crisp white paper
in cheerful fonts.

So instead of writing
and remembering,
I head for the forest,
the pond, the marsh,
where I envy the creatures
who suffer no guilt
or foreknowledge of death.
I blend in and snap away
for here I can stop time,
select what will be in sharp relief,
what will be blurred.

City of Doors

For me, the City of Light
was all about entrances

royal blue gone tough guy
with wrought iron

burst of teal framed
with pink and red geraniums

rusted verdigris gates
tantalizingly ajar

a luxurious, golden invitation
to a sweet shop

sending chocolate fragrance
wafting along the Seine

ornate, pale limestone
of the perfumery

spraying iridescent bubbles
onto the Champs-Élysées.

I longed to enter
each of those doors

and maybe even Pussy's
in dicey Montmartre

with its broad windows
boasting lingerie confections.

I stepped instead
into lush green

at La Closerie des Lilas
where Hemingway wrote

The Sun Also Rises,
took a seat in the garden terrace,

ordered wine in his honor
since it was too early

for absinthe, which to be honest
is not my style at any hour,

and watched a patrician
woman with close-cropped hair

who reminded me
of Lady Brett from the book

blow whorls
of cigarette smoke

toward her male companion.
I caught *when I was young . . .*

as dusk's red cape
settled over the treetops.

Upon Googling an Old Boyfriend and Finding His Obituary

Eleven years ago
he checked outta here,
dead at 58,
just as I emerged
from a cancer chrysalis.

No mention of a wife
or children,
and no more chances
for me to apologize
for stomping on his heart
40 years ago.

The absence of kids
stings a bit
since his mention early on
of having *little Terrys* with me
was what sent me running,
still a little Terry myself.
I wasn't expecting a man
to want to stick around.
Even I didn't care that much
for my company.

I don't remember
breaking up
or explaining anything.
I just stopped
answering my phone,

heard his motorcycle
stirring the summer night
outside my apartment
where I was kissing my new man.
We ran into each other
at the newspaper where we worked,
wound up at the same parties
where his eyes followed me everywhere
and I accepted his cocaine
but nothing else.

He moved to D.C., where I heard he crashed
his motorcycle, struggled with a brain injury,
but in his 20s he was a sun-burnished god,
all muscle and quick to smile.
Good with his hands, he had built
his own catamaran, and we sailed
on the Banana River
and in the Atlantic
amid pods of dolphins.

His sister left a cryptic online remembrance:
Unfortunately, he took the wrong path in life.
So many questions
and no answers.
See, here I go again, making it all about me.

Lemonade

Into the country store she sashayed,
blonde and molded into a peach
sweater, clutching the arm
of my long-haired French mechanic.
Her eggshell-perfect teeth twinkled
as she ordered a turkey and Swiss on rye
with fresh lemonade, and the man
I'd called two nights earlier
to fix my flat did not introduce us.

I'm not proud of what I did.
I was ashamed of my deli uniform—
down-home apron with pockets so large
they could have concealed a voodoo doll
had I known about them then—
and sick of stinking of liverwurst,
pickles and pepper jack cheese.
I wanted to smell like lilies,
with hair that stayed in place,
cashmere and manicured hands
that would never be expected to root
in a grimy trunk for a jack
to change my own damn tire.

Again and again I jumped
on the wrench to loosen the lugs,
wishing it was his neck instead,
while he gave directions and lectured me
about lessons for my own good,

not a gob of grease on his fingers,
men honking horns and shouting
coarse critiques of my ass.

How dare he treat me
like one of the guys then parade
before me Miss Priss, all smooth angles
and condescension till she choked
on the drink into which I'd stirred salt,
burst the dam of her delicate nose,
sprayed a pale-yellow geyser
at the man I fancied, who slapped her
on the back, ran to me for more napkins,
yelped, *Help! My sister's taken ill!*

Mints

Upstairs
in my grandparents' house
in Maine, the room where I slept
during summer visits
was all windows.
Sunlight was the waiter
and kept the Blue Willow tea cups filled
for me and my dolls.

Come darkness
fear caught in my throat
when I came to
if I should die before I wake.
I reached for the powdery, pastel mints
Nana left under my pillow each night
and nestled into innocence.
It held me tight
like favorite pajamas
almost outgrown.

Curtains slapped the window
as I spied on the teenagers below
holding hands and giggling
as they danced home
from the movies
the skating rink
the park.

I couldn't wait to be older,
to taste the cinnamon
of summer nights.
I didn't know it yet
but oh how I would yearn
for the melting candy
of young men.

Friday Nights at the Skating Rink

I hated that first hour
while you watched
your beloved *Star Trek* at home
and I watched the door.

Round and round
went the 45s
in the glass booth
and the gaggles of girls,
pompoms fat as magnolia blossoms
dancing on our white skates
as we swayed to Strawberry Alarm Clock
and Sly and the Family Stone.

At last the jolt of your face
at the ticket window.
You took forever
to lace your skates
and glide onto the rink,
goosebumps thrilling my skin
as you took your place beside me.

The pleasure I had pumped up all day
like a bicycle tire
began to deflate as you detailed
the plot of the night's episode.
I tried not to sigh or roll my eyes
but I loathed Mr. Spock
and the starship *Enterprise*.

When the lights dimmed for a slow skate
and "Crystal Blue Persuasion,"
boys who were accomplished
on the rink had their pick of girls
in whirling, psychedelic skirts.
You could not skate backward well
and I was ungainly
on legs like flower stalks
but we tried for romance anyway.
Love, love is the answer (ooh, ooh).
Our skates clacked and collided,
we struggled to stay upright,
but if I went down,
I took you with me.

Midnight came too soon, and we parted
with hardly a word, embarrassed
by our mothers parked outside
in nightgowns and pink sponge curlers.
All the drive home I replayed
the night, my feet still phantom rolling,
the music my one true love
though I didn't realize it then,
"Apples, Peaches, Pumpkin Pie"
on a syrupy loop, better than
a summer afternoon at the pool
in my hot-pink bikini, better than
a dripping orange Creamsicle at the park,
better than anything I could imagine
as I waited for my sugar
in those sweet, sweet years.

If I Dare

If I dare
say your name
out loud
after all
these years
it's like dropping
a wineglass
from a cliff.
It falls
and falls

but never
hits bottom,
never
shatters.

Memory makes its own glue,
repairs the days
you shrank
from my brash
faith in us,
the nights
I wished
you had more
to say.

The past
won't pass.
We still kiss in cars,

unzip
evening's tight dress,
let it fall.
And fall.
And fall.

About the Author

Terry Godbey is the author of *Hold Still,* a finalist for the Main Street Rag Poetry Book Award; *Beauty Lessons,* winner of the Quercus Review Poetry Book Award; *Behind Every Door,* winner of the Slipstream Poetry Chapbook Contest; and *Flame.* She is also a winner of the Rita Dove Poetry Award. Her poems have been featured in *Rattle, Poet Lore, Crab Creek Review, Rosebud, The Florida Review,* and many other journals. Her work includes a surprising number of windows and doors, and she would no doubt write more if her home did not provide expansive views of dense woods, a pond, and a garden with busy bird feeders. She lives in Orlando, Florida.

Learn more about her and her work at:
terrygodbey.com

www.ingramcontent.com/pod-product-compliance
Lightning Source LLC
Chambersburg PA
CBHW071013160426
43193CB00012B/2030